Colors

Pink

Seeing Pink All around Us

by Michael Dahl

Consulting Editor: Gail Saunders-Smith, PhD

Capstone
press

Mankato, Minnesota

A+ Books are published by Capstone Press,
151 Good Counsel Drive, P.O. Box 669, Mankato, Minnesota 56002.
www.capstonepress.com

1 2 3 4 5 6 10 09 08 07 06 05

Library of Congress Cataloging-in-Publication Data
Dahl, Michael.
    Pink: seeing pink all around us / by Michael Dahl.
    p. cm.—(A+ Books. Colors)
    Includes bibliographical references and index.
    ISBN 0-7368-3670-5 (hardcover)
    ISBN 0-7368-5072-4 (paperback)
    1. Pink—Juvenile literature. 2. Color—Juvenile literature. I. Title. II. Series.
QC495.5.D346 2005
535.6—dc22   2004014352

Summary: Text and photographs describe common things that are pink, including tongues, bubble gum,
    and candy hearts.

Credits
Blake A. Hoena, editor; Heather Kindseth, designer; Kelly Garvin, photo researcher

Photo Credits
All images provided by Capstone Press/Gary Sundermeyer, except for Capstone Press/Karon Dubke, cover; Corbis/Lester
    Leftowitz, 24–25

Note to Parents, Teachers, and Librarians

The Colors books use full-color photographs and a nonfiction format to introduce children to the world
of color. *Pink* is designed to be read aloud to a pre-reader or to be read independently by an early reader.
Photographs and activities help listeners and early readers understand the text and concepts discussed.
The book encourages further learning by including the following sections: Table of Contents, Glossary,
Read More, Internet Sites, and Index. Early readers may need assistance using these features.

Table of Contents

Pink is fluffy.
Pink is frilly.

Taste buds cover the top of your tongue. They let you know if food is sweet, salty, bitter, or sour.

Pink is wet,
and pink is silly.

Piggy banks weren't named after pigs. They were named after "pygg," a type of clay. Hundreds of years ago, people used this clay to make jars to hold coins.

Pink is good for saving money.

9

Pink is sticky.
Pink is funny.

In 1928, Walter Diemer invented bubblegum. He made bubblegum pink because he only had pink food coloring at the time.

Pink is yummy on a stick.

About 100 years ago, cotton candy was called fairy floss.

13

More than 1 billion gallons of ice cream are made in the United States each year. That's enough ice cream to fill a small lake.

Pink is creamy, cool, and thick.

Pink tastes sweet on birthday cakes.

In Russia, many children are given birthday pies instead of cakes. Frosting isn't put on the pies. The pies have messages cut into their crusts.

Early erasers were called "rubbers" because they "rubbed out" pencil marks. People in Great Britain still call erasers by this name.

Pink erases your mistakes.

Pink can blossom.
Pink can bend.

Gerberas are a kind of
daisy that grows in
Africa. They come in
pinks, reds, oranges,
yellows, and whites.

Pink is fun
to give a friend.

Millions and millions of candy
hearts are made each year.
If all of the hearts were
lined up in a row, they would
stretch from New York City
to Los Angeles and back.

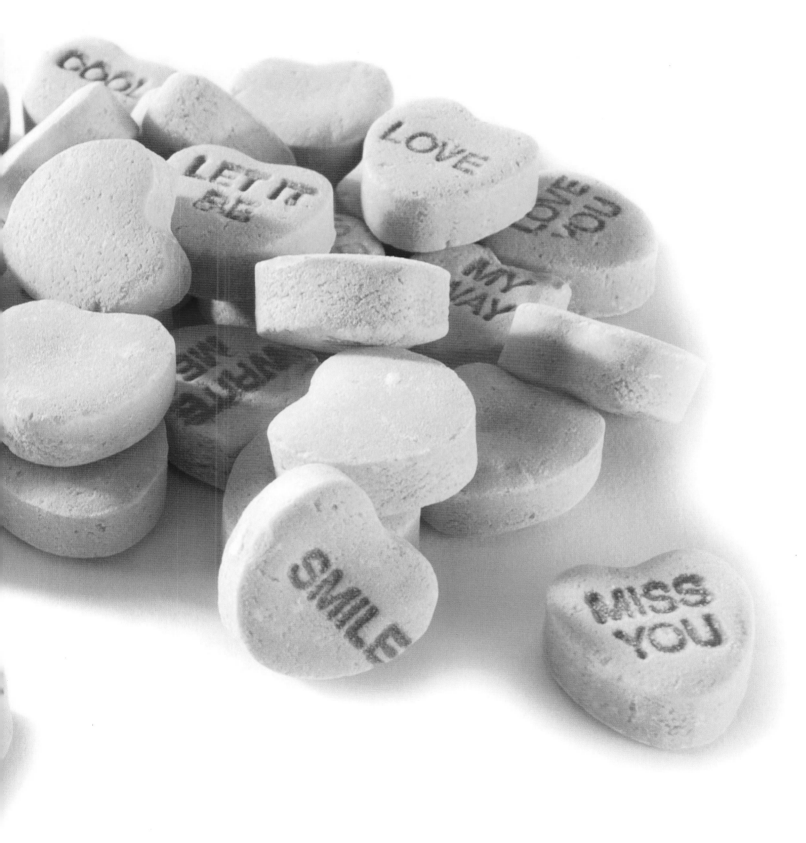

Pink can float
across the sky.

Clouds don't actually turn colors. They look pink, red, or orange at sunrise and sunset because sunlight is reflecting off them.

Pink can hide
a big surprise.

Mixing Pink

Artists mix colors together to create new colors. Pink is made by mixing red and white. Different hues of pink can be made by mixing more or less white with the red.

You will need

paint tray
white paint
red paint
paintbrushes
paper

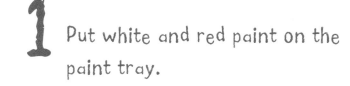

1 Put white and red paint on the paint tray.

2 Use a paintbrush to move a small portion of the red paint to a clean spot on the paint tray. Then mix a small amount of white with the new portion of red. Notice how the red becomes lighter and turns pink. Repeat this step three times. Each time, use a little more white when mixing the paints. What happens?

3 Now that you have created some new colors, begin to paint your masterpiece!

29

Glossary

bitter (BIT-ur)—having a sharp, harsh taste, such as tea or coffee

blossom (BLOSS-uhm)—to grow a flower

crust (KRUHST)—the crisp outer layer of a pie

food coloring (FOOD KUHL-ur-ing)—dye used to change the color
of food

hue (HYOO)—a color or variety of a color

invent (in-VENT)—to think up and make something new

reflect (ri-FLEKT)—to bounce off an object; at sunrise and sunset,
clouds may look pink, red, or orange because rays of sunlight
reflect off them.

sour (SOU-ur)—having a sharp, acidlike taste, such as a lemon

taste bud (TAYST BUD)—one of the small organs on the top of the
tongue that tell people what things taste like

Read More

Brown, Carron, and Ann Montague-Smith. *First Colour Book.*
New York: Kingfisher, 2003.

Lilly, Melinda. *Color.* Read and Do Science. Vero Beach, Fla.:
Rourke, 2004.

Thomas, Isabel. *Pink Foods.* The Colors We Eat. Chicago:
Heinemann, 2004.

Internet Sites

FactHound offers a safe, fun way to find Internet
sites related to this book. All of the sites on
FactHound have been researched by our staff.

Here's how:
1. Visit *www.facthound.com*
2. Type in this special code 0736836705 for age-appropriate
   sites. Or enter a search word related to this book for a more
   general search.
3. Click on the Fetch It button.

FactHound will fetch the best sites for you!

Index

DATE			